SHINE

Secrets of Extraordinary

Executive Assistants

By

Aneeta Pathak

Published by Motivational Press, Inc.
7777 N Wickham Rd, # 12-247
Melbourne, FL 32940
www.MotivationalPress.com

Manufactured in the United States of America.

ISBN: 978-1-62865-091-4

Dedication

The year 2014 has been dedicated to the Secretary and Administrative Assistant and has been declared as The International Year of the Secretary and Administrative Assistant. I am hereby dedicating my first book to all the Secretaries, Administrative Assistants and Executive Assistants around the world.

To my loving, husband Kesh who has helped me in conceiving this book. Thank you again for believing in me.

To my sons, Kayvine and Jay who have been very supportive.

Ann McIndoo, Author of "So You Want To Write", who got this book out of my head and now in yours.

Mishael Patton, my Coach for her kindness, devotion and endless support.

To my highly respected and loving father-in-law Pandit Ramnath Pathak and mother-in-law, Mrs. Binda Pathak

Acknowledgements

Robert Allen for inviting me to his 3-day conference at his residence in San Diego.

Dan Simsiman for his encouragement and continued support.

Susi McCord, Ram Ramadurai, Peter Viris, Jordan Berg, Mazahir Adamjee and Chris Wetter.

To all my fellow EAs & Senior EAs at The Empire Life Insurance Company.

Stuart Ure and Nicole Veilleux for their support and encouragement to move forward.

A big Thank You to Justin Sachs, CEO of Motivational Press and his amazing team for helping me all way through the publishing process and radio shows

Aneeta Pathak was the office manager of the Mauritian branch of the South African Frankipile construction company, which I managed for three years from 2000 to 2002. She was responsible for all facets of the administration of the company, including personnel matters, accommodation of expatriates, organising travel to other parts of the region where the company operated and travel home for expatriates, organising payrolls and correspondence control.

She is an expert in the subject of her book, which can be highly recommended to anyone aiming to be the ideal support for any manager. Without her support during my stay in Mauritius, my life would have been extremely difficult.

Chris C. Wetter
– Construction Management Consultant – South Africa

There are many different work environments that one encounters throughout their career. I had the opportunity to work together with Aneeta in a mid-sized financial institution that could have written the book on "difficult working environments". I have no doubt that this corporate culture stemmed from the executives that were running the show. That being said, Aneeta's ability to deal with these people on a regular basis in an efficient, organized, and pleasant manner shows just how effective an EA she is.

EAs often get overlooked when it comes to recognizing the achievements of the executives to whom they report. Aneeta deserves full marks for truly being a master of the craft.

Jordan Berg
Jordan Berg Consulting - Provider of customized learning solutions
for a wide range of industries

I was delighted to learn that Aneeta is writing a book based on her past experience as an Executive Assistant.

During the time she spent in our Company and as my Personal Assistant, she was an exemplary PA, taking care of correspondences, recording minutes of meetings and assuming all the demanding duties of an Executive Assistant.

She always gave the best of herself and both my colleagues and myself were very satisfied first of all with her work and secondly her dedication and sense of responsibility. Further she always contributed towards creating a convivial environment amongst all the staff.

I wish her plenty of success with her book and I am sure that her book will have plenty of useful tips for all persons starting this career.

Mazahir Adamjee
Former MD Quality Beverages Limited
Bell-Rose, Mauritius

Aneeta is someone that I have been close to for many years. I am drawn to her for her positive energy, strong work ethic and for the empathetic person that she is. Aneeta exudes confidence and is a natural leader. An excellent Executive Assistant is one that completes tasks in an unselfish manner, drawing very little recognition or praise. Yet it would be difficult to ignore Aneeta's efforts when I had the privilege of working with her. It is of no surprise that Aneeta has much to share and a book of this nature only confirms that she is more than just a subject matter expert. I know that I am better not only for having the opportunity of working with Aneeta, but including her in the circle of people that I admire.

Peter Viris
Financial Advisor in Toronto

I first knew Aneeta Professionally and later got to know bits of her personal life.

Aneeta started her career with Generation 5 Mathematical Technologies Inc. as an Administrative support resource to a few key functions in the Organization.; very typical of a medium size enterprise.

Little did we know we had a sudden vacuum with the position of Admin Asst. to the CEO falling vacant!

As was the practice we looked in to see who best could take on this role and it was none other than Aneeta! She was a unanimous choice; for she had the talent to move up!

For starters, Aneeta was apprehensive; which was expected. However, the top team assured her their support and she STOOD up to the challenge. Hours and hours of HARD work, Great attitude, willing to learn, adapt and deliver.

Years gone by but Aneeta made it a point to stay in touch and she is back - Writing a book ! That's GREAT

Ramanan Ramadurai

Independent Consultant/Strategic Solutions Provider
Overland Park, Kansas

Contents

Foreword

by Robert G. Allen

I was delighted when I received a request from Aneeta Pathak to bless her book by writing a foreword for her first book – "Shine – Secrets of Extraordinary Executive Assistant". In October 2013, I met Aneeta and her husband Kesh at my house in San Diego for a 3-day immersion on The Fortune In You. At the end of the conference, Aneeta discovered the fortune within her and today I am so proud about the great book that she has written.

I am amazed at her talents and achievements. This book is a mine of information demonstrating the techniques that she uses in her everyday life as an Executive Assistant. Aneeta is giving back to the community about what she has learned for over more than 25 years during her career. This book is a source of information and inspiration for seasoned and aspiring Executive Assistants.

"Secrets of the Extraordinary Executive Assistants" will teach you her magic and winning formula. Do you want to be portrayed as the committed, detailed-oriented, efficient, fearless, and go-getter by your boss and peers? By using these components, you will learn how to skyrocket your results at the office. At the end of the day, all you have to do is to believe in yourself, be happy and confident.

Aneeta's book is unique and surely a work to be treasured. So, read it, enjoy it and learn from it.

Thank you Aneeta for producing such a great work!

Robert G. Allen
Founder of The Fortune In You

Introduction

Shine – Secrets of Extraordinary Executive Assistants teaches you my magic and winning formula of becoming the extraordinary Executive Assistant (EA) and how to skyrocket your results by using commitment, detail-oriented, efficient, fearless, go-getter; the (CDEFGG) formula which will help you in becoming fearless, disciplined, committed and enthusiastic.

Chapter 1

Choosing My Career Path and My Winning Formula

Sharing with you my winning formula, which I have treasured and respected for over 27 years, brings me tremendous joy. I want to give you access to my blueprint of success which will help you in becoming this special and extraordinary Executive Assistant (EA).As we all know, success varies according to the individual. It is measured in love, money, career, relationships, and this is a never-ending list. An Executive Assistant (EA) will make every effort to be successful in their career.

Excel in what you do and success will follow.

This is one of my favorite inspiring quotes, which I read every day before starting anything. This is a ritual for me to stay focused: excel in what you do and success will follow. Breathe in your personal life, breathe in your professional life, focus on what you do, and excel in the tasks that you undertake.

Are you eager to read more about my winning formula? You already know the formula, but now and then, you just need someone to tinkle the little bell in your ears to remind you about it.The ABC of this winning formula is to be aware of your CDEFGG. Oh, well! You are trying to figure out about cracking this code. My formula is sweet and simple; however, I would like <u>YOU</u> to ask yourself these five main questions:

1. Am I Committed?

2. Am I Detail-Oriented?

3. Am I Efficient?

4. Am I Fearless?

5. Am I a Go-Getter?

I am convinced that, you all have the CDEFGG within you, and I would like to go deeper into each drop of this formula to help you to either discover or enliven the diamond within you. *As Confucius said, "The will to win, the desire to succeed, the urge to reach your full potential . . . these are the keys that will unlock the door to personal excellence."*

One of my favorite quotes from Mahatma Gandhi: "The future depends on what we do in the present." Actually, I think this quote relates well to me. This short story will give you a better idea about my career path and me.

I think that my entire career path was pre-determined when I was ten years old: organizing parties for my friends, planning the logistics, sending out invitations, negotiating for discounts at the birthday stores, and the list goes on. Every time my mother wanted to organize a big family lunch or dinner, she always came to me for ideas about planning and organizing any events.

After high school, I attended a two-year course on Secretarial Duties at ORIAN institute, one of the best schools for Secretaries in Mauritius.

Some of you might still remember those days when we had to study shorthand. Wikipedia describes shorthand as "an abbreviated symbolic writing that increases speed and brevity of writing as compared to a normal method of writing a language." Shorthand was used more widely in the past before the invention of recording and dictation machines. When I completed my two-year secretarial course, I got my first job as a secretary in a driving school that I enjoyed very much because I learned how to anticipate the needs of my boss and felt that I was the backbone of this organization. It was not just administrative work but within a few weeks I learned how she thinks, what were her expectations from me and my goal was to make my executive successful. Hence, I made up my mind and was determined to pursue my career as an Executive Assistant.

Chapter 2

Commitment

"Stay committed to your decisions, but stay flexible in your approach."

—*Quote from Tony Robbins*

Are you genuinely committed?

- As parents towards your kids.

- As a doctor towards your patients.

- To your boss and the organization you work for.

High Level of Commitment

A high-level of commitment is required for being a competent and efficient Executive Assistant and you have to be truthfully committed. When you have to complete a task on your to-do list or your boss has requested your help on a project, ensure that your willingness to complete that task or project is coming straight from your heart. Feel the satisfaction and experience it, every time you complete a task on your to-do list or when your boss praises you for a well-done job. When you are committed to your work, you accept no excuses, only results.

Contributing to effective relationships and understanding others also shows your commitment to your work environment. Be a role model of behavior.

Punctuality

The rule of the game is to be on time at the office every day. Let us talk about punctuality. How many times do you snooze your alarm clock in the morning? Once, twice, or thrice. We all know how difficult it is to wake up in the morning! Oh my God! Sleeping is so good! But remember, you have to be a responsible person. I know you must be saying to yourself, "we know we are responsible." But you know what? From time to time, you need someone to remind you to be responsible.

Earlier I asked about how many times you hit snooze on your alarm clock. Always try your best to be on time at the office. Be at the office ten or fifteen minutes earlier. This will give you a little moment to organize yourself before the show starts and be ready to face a day full of challenges. We all know that an EA's day cannot be complete without having to face any challenges.

We have a daily plan of how our day will go at the office. However, there are times we see ourselves in situations where the plans have changed. Hence, we have to be prepared and ready for the changes. Being on time consistently demonstrates foresight, the ability to envisage possible problems. Moreover, by being flexible, you have the ability to change your plans to accommodate those problems.

You wake up one morning with a terrible headache; this is when you become aware that you will be late at the office. Inform your boss as soon as possible—send him/her an email. It does not matter whether it is four or five in the morning. Nowadays, all bosses are equipped with the latest technology, so a quick email to them is a nice way to let them know you will show up late at the office. Why do you think you have to inform them about your tardiness at the office? It is because you care for them; but it is not only about caring—you are concerned about your work as well, because you are a responsible person.

Punctuality shows you value people; you show them respect. Everyone is busy and you would not like them to be waiting on you, and their work goes unattended. Being late at the office has a negative impact to ongoing projects.

You are working with a team on a project; you are late at the office and they are waiting for you, as they need your input on certain subjects. You do not even care to notify them; this clearly sends an image of unprofessionalism and irresponsibility.

Try to predict your commute time. Observe the average duration of your commute; give yourself extra time by watching weather and traffic reports. Plan to be on time and make punctuality a priority.

Punctuality conveys a positive signal to your boss and your peers. It shows that you are dedicated to your job and capable of handling responsibilities. Always be on time at work or any work-related activity; being punctual, projects a sense of professionalism and commitment. Punctuality shows reliability and trust. One of the ways to build other people's trust in you is by consistently meeting your commitments and this starts by being punctual.

Unpunctuality leads to stress and your performance is affected. Remember, when tardiness becomes the pattern, your job might be in jeopardy.All of us have heard or may have experienced Murphy's Law; so watch out as it is very likely that your boss might be waiting for you to give him/her a document that they need for an impromptu meeting.

I always do my best to be on time at the office. It so happened that one day I left home a little bit later than usual. I went to my regular coffee shop; the line was quite long and I was not worried at all about the time. I was very certain that I would still be at my desk on time. Unfortunately, on that day, I showed up late at the office. My boss was waiting for me impatiently, as she had forgotten her password to log into her computer. Will you ever think that your boss can forget a log in password! Yes indeed, they do forget as well, and that is why we are to help them remember. We need to understand the pressures our bosses are going through and find a way to alleviate their stresses.

We all know that most of the executives are early birds; they are always the first ones to show up in the morning. This is an example of how punctuality reflected on my image once. It so happened that one day, around 8:00am, the CEO was calling my boss. He had to schedule an impromptu meeting, and the latter has not yet arrived, and of course, since I was already at the office, I took this call on behalf of my boss. The CEO sounded pleasantly surprised because I was there to take his call and at the same time, he asked me to schedule the unplanned meeting. We all know how time is of the essence for all executives; answering that call and assisting the CEO has conveyed a message of punctuality.

You can be late; let us say there is a subway delay, bad weather conditions—this is comprehensible. However, do not make it a habit, like, "I'll wake up in a few minutes. Let me hit snooze on my alarm clock." Then, when you get up, you are in a rush and realize how late you are. You want to get to the office as fast as possible; your mind is upset and you cannot think straight. As we all know, being late at the office does not help at all. Thomas C. Haliburton once said, "Punctuality is the soul of business."

Respecting deadlines

"Deadlines aren't bad. They help you organize your time. They help you set priorities. They make you get going when you might not feel like it."

– Quote from Harvey Mackay

As an Executive Assistant (EA) you are aware of your duty and responsibility vis-à-vis your boss and the organization you work for. You are also conscious that any project assigned to you has to be completed and delivered within a certain target date.

Above all, ensure that you know about all deadlines that are assigned to your boss. Key in these dates into his/her calendar and in yours as well. Check if the documents have to be reviewed by other people before your boss finalizes them. Always make a note of outside factors into your due date timeline (such as postage or couriers, for example) and ensure the requested deadlines do not coincide with your boss's vacation plans. Moreover, have a reminder in both calendars two days prior to the due date—sometimes there are other meetings being cancelled, and you can remind your boss to use this free time slot to work on the task that will be due soon.

To become the successful and extraordinary EA, you have to be prepared, flexible, and proactive. Think ahead and try to plan. Anticipate problems and try to solve them. Come with solutions and not problems. Trust me—your boss, peers, and other executives will perceive you as a great EA because you have already proven to them that you are a problem-solver. Set your own expectations; know what you want to achieve. Keep your expectations realistic because there is nothing more frustrating or discouraging than spending time sorting out a new plan, only to find that it will not work.

Prioritize your work. Keep track of dates and occasions. Analyze your accomplishments every day. Make every effort to complete assignments promptly. Do not linger until the last minute and then drive the rest of your co-workers crazy by asking for help to catch up.

Set up a fake deadline for any tasks that you have to deliver. I know that many of you do not like the idea of "setting up fake deadlines," because you feel like you are being pressured. Let's put it like this: you have to work on a project that is due in one week's time. Go ahead and set up the fake cut-off date in your calendar. This exercise will give you ample time to concentrate. If you have completed the project within two days prior to the delivery date, you will be more comfortable to review it again. Re-visit your grammar, verbs, punctuations, and spelling. If you are working on an Excel spreadsheet, ensure that you have the correct formulas in your document.

If you think that you will not be able to respect a certain deadline due to other urgent priorities, there is one thing that you can do when confidentiality is involved in the task on which you are working. We all know that an EA deals with a lot of confidential subjects. Find out from your boss if you can ask for help from another EA. It will be fair if you let your boss know that given the circumstances of so many things happening within the department, you feel that you will not be able to complete a certain task for the prescribed deadline. This is how I approach my boss in this kind of situation: *"I do not see myself handing over project E to you next Tuesday, given that project B is your priority now. I will try my best but do you think I can ask Lisa to help me".*If you let your boss know that most likely, you might not be in a position to meet that cutoff date, there is high probability that he/she might extend the deadline because they have been forewarned. By giving a heads-up to your boss, you can consider yourself secured and your boss will have two options; either extend the deadline or agree that you get help from another Executive Assistant.I would like to share with you some tips that I use in managing deadlines:

- Always nail down all due dates both in your boss's calendar and in your calendar as well.

- Set up a fake deadline, normally I have it two days prior to the due date.

- Check if your boss has any planned vacations or is planning to take any vacations during that time.

- Make sure you ask for a date and time for the deadline. Never take ASAP or URGENT as a deadline because this will not help you to realign your priorities effectively and efficiently.

- Understand that there are consequences if you do not meet your deadline. And in the end, you will look unprofessional and disorganized.

- If you are looking for specific documents with other Executives, always provide them with the date and time you need it. As an EA, remember to send them a friendly reminder one day before the due date. For those using Outlook as a means of sending emails, always include the "reminder" option with the date and time. I love this feature because when the time is due, the reminder pops up and you cannot miss it.

- Plan how you will meet your deadline. Whether on your calendar or any other system you have, it does not matter as long as you do have a plan to get the work done. If this is a big project, try to break the task into smaller sections and make sure to mark each stage in your calendar until you reach the final stage of the project.

- If you know that you will not be able to hit the deadline, let the person know well in advance. Maybe you can ask for an extension or try to realign your priorities.

- Never wait to the last minute to run after an important deadline.

Demands and expectations from management can change rapidly. Projects are adjusted and sometimes deadlines are moved up. This is why you have to set up fake deadlines. Flexibility is the name of the game in adjusting to changes in deadlines without letting them affect your productivity or quality of work. You have to be flexible—to be organized and prepared in advance. You have to be flexible, organized and prepared in advance.

I would like to tell you about one of my experiences related to "Respecting Deadlines". I had a three-week timeframe to revise the quarterly report. I had to check on grammar, verbs, punctuations, formatting, consistency... Moreover, I also had to take care of my regular daily chores and to expect the unexpected. Everything was going on well as planned when I received an email from my boss asking me to get everything set up in two days for an ad hoc Board of Director meeting. "Oh jeez," I just wanted to run away. After reading that email, I went for a quick walk to unwind and came back with a new perspective. Of course, the Board of Directors meeting could not wait.

Therefore, I approached my boss with two solutions for this situation.
1. Seek help from another EA to finalize the quarterly report.
2. Ask if we could extend the delivery date by two days.
And it was decided that we would go with solution number 2.

Every now and then, you have to judge and differentiate between important and urgent. In this case, the Board of Directors was urgent. Every challenging situation is an opportunity to show your boss how flexible you are to changes.

Reliability

"We are sure to get opportunities as we show ourselves capable of being trusted."

—Quote from Roy L. Smith

How reliable are we as an Executive Assistant?

Reliability is a personality trait, which is considered very important. In short, reliability is the quality of being honest and trustworthy to the organization you work for, your boss, your peers, and anyone around you. The importance of reliability is that it allows people to trust you to do the things you say you are going to do, and to rely on you when they need you.

Being a reliable EA forms part of a good work ethic. To be reliable means to be consistent regardless of the amount of extra effort it takes. If you are that reliable EA, you would like to take certain steps and actions to allow yourself to be totally reliable. Punctuality is one of the examples that we can use to define reliability. Punctuality is a sign of respect, which makes you look good and dependable. This is when your boss will know that they can turn to you, knowing that you are reliable and performing consistently.

Most Executive Assistants will show their worth to the organization at a very early stage. They do not take unnecessary sick leaves, and always plan to have a backup before going on vacation for a long period. Be genuine. Do not fake your personality. Just be yourself.

Another great way to be a reliable EA is to be the person who is good at his/her job. Always remember, that you do not have to know how to do everything, but you should be able to perform your core job. We learn every day; every situation we run into during the day is a learning opportunity. Sometimes, we hesitate to ask questions; we always try to guess. **NO**, you have to stop guessing, because being able to ask questions to do the job right is something that will make you reliable. To be a reliable EA is about changing your attitude and aligning your needs and objectives towards the organization you work for.Here are some key ingredients you can use to add to your reliability recipe that will help you in becoming this reliable Executive Assistant:

- Always be on time.
- Be willing to take on challenges.
- Leave the gossip to others.
- Perform your job with zero error or nominal error.
- Be responsible and your boss will know that they can count on you.
- Take responsibility for your actions.
- Try to display exceptional performance day after day.
- Do not get derailed by obstacles and pressures.
- Be honest when you say "Yes" and "No".

When mistakes are made, many people are reluctant to apologize, fearing that admitting fault will harm their reputation or be perceived as stupid. To be honest is the best way to repair a situation.

If you know that you have made a mistake when sending an email to executive members of the organization, inform your boss immediately. Let him/her know that you can solve the issue; you are sending an apology note informing them about the mistake, and you are taking care of it. You will feel less stressed after sending that apology note. Your boss and the executive members will see you as someone accountable. This is when you will increase their trust level in you.

When establishing some kind of routines in your working style, you will have the feeling of becoming more and more reliable. Your boss and peers will perceive this touch of reliability in you.For example, I set up routines when scheduling meetings. Let us say there is a bi-weekly recurrent meeting. To begin with, I will check the availability of the members. As we know, usually it is not that simple to have everyone available at the same time. This is where we will use our good judgment. If out of ten members, six members can make it, we will ask the other four members if they can change their schedules to make themselves available.I will send an email to the attendees and provide them with pertinent information, such as time, occurrence, and any preparation required from each member prior to the meeting. Also, let them know that you checked their availabilities and noticed that out of ten members; only four of them have conflicts. And that it will be great if those 4 members can manage their schedules and become available.

This is a bi-weekly meeting held on Wednesdays and as per the Chair's requirements; the agenda and reading materials are to be forwarded to the members by 12 pm, 2 days prior to the meeting. If the agenda and reading materials have to reach the members forty-eight hours before the meeting, this indicates that all documents must reach the members at least by 12pm on Friday. For sake of understanding, I'll use a fictitious date – let's say the meeting is on Wednesday February 12, 2014

- On Monday, February 3rd, ask members to send the agenda items they would like to table at next week's meeting and that I expect to receive all documentation by 5:00pm. On Wednesday, February 5th. Thursday, February 6th, compile all documents and prepare the agenda.Check if any members have declined the meeting. BBy 2:00pm on February 6th get everything ready for the Chair's approval. On Friday, February 7th morning prior to sending by email the meeting documents, check the following:

- Reading materials have been spell-checked and attached to the email.

- Meeting time, location, and name of meeting room clearly and correctly indicated on the agenda.
- The Chairperson has been notified of any absences.
- Check that you have the correct email addresses of the attendees.

You no longer have to worry about forgetfulness if you adopt a routine way of checking any tasks that are assigned to you.Make it a priority to be the reliable Executive Assistant. If you want to be known as someone reliable, be true to your commitments and establish routines.

Dedication

"Any job very well done that has been carried out by a person who is fully dedicated is always a source of inspiration."

—Quote from Carlos Ghosn

We all know that it is a fact that most people do not like their jobs and wish they did not have to wake up every morning to go to work. However, you must know whether you like your job or not, and if you are a dedicated employee. However, do you think that dedication is just showing up for work every day? One can say, "Yes, I am a dedicated employee because I work forty hours per week and sometimes more depending on my work load." Moreover, I believe that dedication is so much more than that.

An important factor that your boss looks for in you is dedication. Being a dedicated EA on the job, you will ensure that your boss receives the very best from you and that the job is carried out to the best of your ability. Take real pride in the job you do and become an expert in what the job entails. One of the great things you can do for your company's success, and your job security, is to know what your company needs from you and what you will do for the company you work for. You will do anything to ensure that you perform well. Sometimes you will put in extra hours beyond what is expected, because you want to get the job done. It is not only that you want to get that task completed; but also you want to look good vis-à-vis your boss.

How many times do you walk the extra mile?

- Working during lunchtime—there is an impromptu meeting and you have to get everything ready for your boss to attend this meeting.

- Reaching home after a tiring day at the office—your boss calls and asks you to make an urgent travel arrangement, because they have to be on the first flight to London tomorrow morning.

- Staying after office hours to help your boss complete a major project.

- Exceeding expectations, this is what a devoted and dedicated EA does. If the need arises, he/she will show up very early, stay late and even take work home. Most of the Executive Assistants do understand that sometimes it takes extra effort to get a task done for a deadline. Also, remember they are not likely to ask for additional praise or compensation for the extra effort and time because they are naturally committed to getting their job done accurately and in a timely manner.

- A diligent EA will respect company time and make it a point to remain genuinely busy while on the clock. They will avoid wasting time with small talk or hanging around the water cooler.

- A dedicated EA will look ahead to ensure that he/she is prepared for upcoming duties and events.

If you are still smiling after walking those extra miles, consider yourself a dedicated and committed Executive Assistant—"give yourself a pat on the back".Always remember that your enthusiastic attitude is one of the key elements that will make you rise and shine, and be portrayed as the exceptional Executive Assistant.Put your best foot forward and be ready to help your boss and peers. Remember to pay attention when your boss talks to you. Always have a notebook on you, just in case you have to jot down some notes. It is rare that a person waits and listens before carrying out any directives. By listening carefully and without interruption to your boss, mistakes can be eliminated. When they are done talking and if you have any questions or need to clarify certain points, this will be a good time to ask your questions. It also shows respect to your superior, and will not go unnoticed. Work with assurance and confidence. Be proud of yourself each time your boss praises you for a well-done job.

Dedication means always wearing a smile; treat your peers as you would like to be treated. If your peers are in a bad mood, do not let their moods rub off on you. Instead, maintain positive thinking, positive actions, and be happy. This is the key to infusing the full sense of dedication into your work life.Sometimes it is difficult to maintain positive thinking and be happy when you are having a bad day. A bad day may be because commuting was awful, or you could not get your favorite coffee. Sometimes it could be a small issue or it could be a big problem. As an EA, try to learn how to keep work and life separate because most likely, your performance will be affected, and your boss's expectations are for you to work effectively and efficiently. However, if you are having a big personal issue, the best thing to do is to talk about it to your boss and let them know that you will try your best not to let this problem interfere with your work and that you really appreciate them being supportive of you.

Be the dedicated EA that every boss wants to have. We are not born with traits of dedication, but we can learn and cultivate how to be a dedicated human being at home and at work.

Continuous Learning for Personal Development

"Never become so much of an expert that you stop gaining expertise. View life as a continuous learning experience."
—*Quote from Denis Waitley*

We live and work in a society depending on technology, and we have to keep abreast of technological changes and quickly master new technology. If your boss is not too tech-savvy, he/she will look for you when having trouble formatting a file while using the latest version of Microsoft Office for Word, Excel, or Power Point. You will be the one to show them how to do it. And trust me; they will be amazed when they see how simple it is to use the new technical tools.

Keeping up to date with the latest Microsoft Office Suite will show that you easily adapt to changes. As an EA, it is our duty to be a fast learner; to always be on top, and be ready to help our boss whenever there is a new system that has been implemented. We have to continue learning for our self-improvement and to help our boss when he/she is having trouble with a newly implemented program.

We all want to grow in our jobs and to keep on growing and succeeding; we have to learn new skills. The more skills we acquired, the more value we can offer to our boss. Become "the best" at what you do; continue to learn and work on your skills and talents, so that they become highly regarded by your boss and peers. An EA has to know everyone who is at the executive level in the company. If your boss is not around, you can speak on their behalf. What I meant by "speaking on their behalf" is that you have to find time to know on which critical project your boss is working and get familiar to the terminology he/she use in their emails. And if someone asks you a question in their absence, you will be in a position to respond.

Browse the company website and intranet. Show an interest to know what is happening around you. When do we usually browse a company's website? When we have an interview with XYZ Company, then we go on their website and try to learn more about the goals and objectives of the company, so that we can sound knowledgeable and make a great impact during the interview process. However, when you are hired, and start working, you will not be so interested in browsing the company's website due to lack of time and you will think that this is not one of your major priorities. I strongly believe that you have to find time, at least ten minutes each day to riffle through the company's website and intranet, because they are updated on a regular basis. This is your world. Be aware of what is happening around you because you never know who at the executive level might ask if you remember when and where the Annual Meeting for Employees is taking place—so better to be on your guard.

At the end of the day, we all know that we can get on top of our job and field of expertise through continuous learning and personal development. Train your brain to adapt to new methods and techniques that will make you more efficient and effective in your job and at the same time help your boss.

One of the techniques that I use when checking my boss's email is to use the flags option to tag his/her emails with the following remarks: AP (these are my initials.) "AP to take care of," "your immediate action is required," "to read at one's leisure," "personal," "human resources," "to provide comments XX date (calendar has been updated)," "for your e-approval." These email techniques will help your boss to concentrate on other critical requests they have to attend to personally.

In addition to the technical skills required to do your job, you also need to focus on improving your hard skills and soft skills.

Hard skills - related to professional knowledge, tools, or techniques that allow us to work within our profession and to stay competitive:

- Emails and calendar management—these are the basic and paramount tools.

- Office Suite programs—Microsoft Office, which includes Word, Excel, PowerPoint Access, PDF Writer—we need to understand each application and know how to use them.

- Company specific software—such as a software used internally to order office supplies or marketing products.

- Scanners, photocopiers, printers, fax machines—nowadays all four functions come together into a single multi-functional device. Dedicate some time to learn about their specific functions and the troubleshooting process as well, because you will be the one your boss will call if the device is jammed.

Soft skills are the complete collection of our social, communication, and self-management behaviors and are related to personality development:

- **Strong Work Ethic** – Are you committed and dedicated to getting the job done?

- **Positive Attitude** – Are you confident?

- **Good Communication Skills** – Are you verbally articulate and a good listener?

- **Time Management** – Do you know how to prioritize and work on multiple projects at the same time?

- **Problem Solving skills** – Do you have solutions for every problem you come across?

- **Team Player** – Do you work well in a group?

- **Self-Confidence** – Do you truly believe you can do the job?

- **Acknowledging your mistakes** – Do you accept that it's your fault when you make mistakes?

- **Accept and learn from criticism** – Can you handle criticism?

- **Adaptability** – Are you able to adapt to changes?

- **Working under pressure** – Can you handle stressful situations where deadlines are important to respect?

This is one of my personal experiences, which I want to share with you.

One of my weaknesses is PowerPoint, which I have to use on a weekly basis to prepare presentations for my boss. I found an online PowerPoint course, convinced my boss that it was worth investing in this program. Here I am now, doing presentations like a pro. This course has helped me tremendously in improving the presentations for my boss, and she was impressed. By identifying a suitable training course, this has also helped me in the preparation for my annual performance appraisal.

If you are equipped with the necessary skills and knowledge, you will be portrayed as the extraordinary Executive Assistant, and this will help you to rise and shine in your career.

Passion

> *"Pleasure in the job puts perfection in the work."*
> —*Quote from Aristotle*

"Tell me about a time when you had an urgent project that could not be completed by the end of your normal workday? What was the situation and what did you do?" —This is one of the favorite questions asked by the hiring manager when you go for a job interview. This question will demonstrate how passionate you are about your job.

Passion is one of the key ingredients that will help you to achieve your goals, and become the successful Executive Assistant. And we all know the recipe for success is passion. Be committed to your passion because a passionate EA is an engaged employee.

Passion is the strong feeling of genuine enthusiasm that is within you. That enthusiasm is so powerful when combined with your work, because you are preparing yourself to walk the path of success. Inject passion in every aspect of your work.

Passion is so important because when you are enthusiastic and proud of the work you do, you are better prepared to surmount the obstacles that will certainly arise in your day-to-day work. The more devoted you are to your job, the more willing you are to work harder at improving yourself.

Always be passionate about your job, not only when working on a great project. Will you feel bad if your boss asks you to go and get coffee for them? Based on my previous experience, I have had quite a few of my peers who were somewhat upset when their bosses asked them to go and get them a cup of coffee. They thought of this as a menial task. There is no little job. No task is too big or too small for the unique EA. Understand that creating expense reports and going to the coffee shop to buy coffee are two equally important tasks that will enable your executive to succeed. Both creating a great expense report and buying a cup of coffee will be extremely helpful for your boss. The expense report will be helpful in tracking all types of expenses and the caffeine will boost their energy level. Let me share with you one of my anecdotes. In one of my previous jobs, when I was a newbie, one of my colleagues called me and said, "There is some clean-up to be done in the meeting room. The management team had a lunch meeting. When you have some time, can you please drop by and take care of the room?" I was somewhat upset, and thought that because I recently joined the company that was why she asked me to clean the meeting room. Then I said to myself, why should I be upset if I have to clean a room—would my reaction have been different if I were asked to take notes during that management meeting?

After going through this situation, I realized that one does not need to have a "big" job to be passionate. A "big" job is not about paperwork or attending a meeting where you want others to see what you are doing. Even though you have to buy a cup of coffee or clean up after an executive lunch meeting, put passion in it. Show respect to whatever type of job you are doing. Talk with passion and excitement, but remember it is not enough that you feel the passion, but let your boss know how passionate you are about your job.

How can you let your boss know about your passion for your job? Yes, you can do that during your one-on-one meetings with your boss. This is where you will show how passionate you are. This is the only time when it is only you and your boss, so you have to let them know that you are very passionate about your job and that you are willing to help on very much, and that you are willing to help on any future projects they are planning to work on. Let them know that you want to grow, you want to learn, and that you want to stay in that company. Passion triggers a lot of enthusiasm, a lot of motivation, and you will feel like you can tackle more tasks without any difficulty. When you are passionate and committed, you will see how the day flies and will be happy about the contribution you have brought throughout the day. Always wear a smile when you talk to your peers or anyone across the organization. You know how you feel when you leave the office after an exhausting day. Even though you are exhausted, you feel happy and surrounded by energetic and positive vibes.

Here are some take-aways that I would like you to use, to unleash the passion within you:

- Identify all essential tasks that you must tackle each day to get the job done. Focus on the tasks that you are more passionate about as passion intensifies your focus. Passion allows you to become more creative. If you are passionate about preparing presentations using Power point, at some point you will notice that you will start having brilliant ideas and this will make your presentations different from others.

- Passion provides you the momentum to persevere and to pursue excellence. If you are passionate about planning off-site meetings, you will find yourself full of energy and will be determined to do an excellent job.

- Passion is infectious. Seek out and spend more time around those people who make you feel more energized, enthusiastic, and passionate.

- Pursuing the passion you have for your job will help you to overcome fear. Afraid of changes? For example, having a new boss or supporting an additional boss. If you are truly passionate about your job, fear is not an option.

I believe that when we are passionate about the work we do, we have more energy to work much harder. We get more creative and are in a better position to search for solutions when problems arise and we inspire others who work next to us.I adopted this quote from Emile Coue as my daily mantra—"Every day, in every way, I'm getting better and better".

Chapter 3

Detail-Oriented

"The difference between something good and something great is attention to detail."

—Quote from Charles R. Swindoll

Are we born with the traits of being very attentive to all details we come across? Whether it is small or negligible? On the other hand, do we have to train ourselves to adopt this second nature? A detail-oriented person is someone who pays a great deal of attention to details.Giving proper attention to details in your work will show you how to attain the path of excellence. When you show your boss that you notice the little things, they will understand that you can handle things on your own and can work with minimal supervision.

If you are dedicated to paying attention to details, you can certainly keep up with your schedules; provide quality work that might not require re-working, meet your deadlines and make your boss's life easier.An Executive Assistant constantly demonstrates their skills of being a detail-oriented person. In other words, I prefer to say that he/she must have the "eagle eyes". An EA must pay attention to everything they write, read, and say; that is, they have to be accurate, consistent, and logical.Always have a notepad on you when talking to your boss. Jotting down notes will help you understand your boss's expectations. This will help you to prioritize your tasks. Make a checklist for everything you have to take care of and remember to check them off to ensure you have not missed any subject.

Attention to details may translate into better working habits and opportunities. Be resistant to lack of time and concentration; these are the factors that will prevent you from reviewing your work before handing it over to your boss or before you set it aside as complete. Ensure to review your work more than once to assure desired completion.Here are some take-aways that will help you in staying focused and paying attention to details, just in case you are losing interest when there are too many details to focus on:

Pay Attention – Avoid multi-tasking when your boss is talking to you, make sure you grasp everything they tell you. What I usually do when he/she is done, I write down all the important points I have captured and make a summary. I read it once or twice to ensure that I have understood the message and the logic behind the message. If I feel that I have missed something, I go back immediately to my boss to summarize things. And of course, if this was not the intended message, I will give myself a second chance to ensure capturing the correct message

Take Notes – It is a good idea to have a notebook on you every time you talk to your boss. You know that every time you address a specific subject to your boss, it always turns out that at the end of the conversation you will emerge with many different subjects to look at. If you do not have a notebook on you, it will be very difficult to remember the outcome of the subject you went to discuss and the additional subjects that your boss asked you take care of.

Ask, ask, and always ask – I believe that sometimes we are afraid to ask for further information and we try to guess, because of two reasons:

1) We do not want our bosses to see us as someone who does not know what to do.

2) We do not like the look they gave us when asking the same information for a second time, because sometimes you feel like either you are stupid or your question is totally incomprehensible.

Neither point # 1 nor # 2 should be an obstacle when you have to go to your boss for more information or clarification about a task that you have been assigned to take care of. Always ask questions to ensure clarity and remember that at the end of the day you have to support your boss, no matter what mood he/she is in.Most of the time, we are provided with ample instruction and information to complete the task. If the instructions are still not clear in your mind or if you need more information, just ask. Ask your boss to provide you with more details so that you will be more effective in delivering a top-notch job.

Relax – Do you know that paying too much attention can be difficult for you to detect the details you are looking for? It is essential to take a quick break from time to time. Taking a break is important; it takes only a few seconds or minutes and then it is easier to focus on your task when you get back. Walk away from your desk, go get yourself a coffee or have a quick chat with a co-worker if he/she is not busy. The point in taking a quick break is to rest your mind so that you are better prepared for the task ahead.

Remember that paying attention to details and raising concerns will give you the opportunity to earn the trust of your boss because they can count on you in spotting errors and correcting any inaccuracies.

Keeping Your Boss on Schedule

It is all about how you spend time managing your day and at the same time keeping track of your boss's priorities and schedules. Taking care of two calendars or multiple calendars is really a challenging task. Office Outlook or Google Calendar is an almighty tool that helps us to plan effectively our boss's day. If you are newly appointed, one of the best things you can do is to read his/her calendar for the previous two or three months to learn about their daily routine. Search for individual or group meetings that they regularly have. For example, meetings with his/ her direct reports. Without prying, make note of personal items on their calendar, such as how often they go to the hairdresser, gym, or take their pet to the veterinary.

As an Executive Assistant, how well you keep your boss's calendar could make the difference between having a poor performance review and having an outstanding performance review. We all know that one of the main tools our bosses use extensively is Outlook, Google Calendar, or some other new system that helps them to keep track of their meetings. Coordinating schedules is a challenge faced by many Executive Assistants every day. Hence, it is crucial to have a good way to view individual calendars in order to effectively manage tasks and plan meetings.

It requires many steps in scheduling meetings for busy executives. This is not only about scheduling a time and a location, but often you have to prepare an agenda, arrange for equipment, and send reminders. Your main objective is to set up meetings that fit into everyone's day. Here are some tips that will help you to better manage your boss's calendar.

- Shared calendars will save you time and help you to better manage your boss's schedules efficiently. If you are supporting multiple executives, ask them to give you access to their respective calendars.

- Every afternoon before leaving the office, print two copies of the daily schedule for the next day. Keep one copy on your desk and give the other copy to your boss. Briefly summarize what their day will look like tomorrow.

- Avoid booking back-to-back meetings, because you know that most of the meetings never end on time. Give your boss an extra ten minutes before scheduling the next one.

- Ensure no double booking of meetings as this will drive your boss crazy and you will look inefficient.

- Double check the name and email addresses of the invitees, as very often you have people with the same first names.Never send a meeting invite before checking the availability of the invitees.

- Check if the meeting room is available and if it can accommodate the number of members invited.

- Check if your boss or any other members will need a projector/ whiteboard during the meeting.

- If your boss has a presentation to make, ensure the projector or any other devices are functioning properly, at least half an hour before the meeting.

- Include your full office address when inviting external clients to a meeting and add a contact number just in case they cannot find the location.

- If meetings are taking place during lunchtime, let the members know that lunch will be provided and to inform you of any food allergies they might have.

- Always remember to check the time zones if you have to set up a conference call or video conference meeting with members in another country or province.

- When scheduling a meeting for your boss to discuss any subjects related to Human Resources, always remember to mark the meeting as private, because you would not like for everyone to see what meeting your boss is attending.

- Have an updated list of fire drill sessions that take place during the year and key in those dates both in your calendar as well as in your boss's calendar. Hence, you will avoid scheduling meetings during that specific time. If your boss has to attend an off-site meeting with a new client, always remember to include the address and contact number of the person your boss is going to meet. Print a Google map with the directions for them. (Keep a copy for your records, as this will help you when submitting mileage claims for your boss.)

- Sometimes it is hard for your boss to remember the vacation plans of his/her direct reports. What I usually do is to mark on their calendar the dates on which their team will be on vacation. By doing this, my boss can anticipate any critical meetings they would like to schedule prior to the team going on vacation.

- On a monthly basis, check with your boss to see if they have any vacation plans. If yes, update their calendar accordingly and at the same time let their direct reports know about your boss's plans, in case they require anything before the vacation.

- Nail down in their calendar the due dates for submission of any quarterly or financial reports/professional membership fees. I usually give my boss a two-day notice in his calendar prior to the actual due date.

- Let your boss know that if you go on vacation or call in sick, they need to copy you of any meeting requests that they will be scheduling in your absence. By doing this, you will be in a better position to follow up on any reminders that you might have to send out prior to those meetings.

- Always have little notes to yourselves jotted in your calendar. Let's say you will be organizing an off-site meeting in three months and you just got an idea on how you will prepare the agenda—write it down right away in your calendar. Because you will not be able to remember the same idea in one-month. Never procrastinate on updating your notes, adding new notes, or reminders to your own calendar.

What is on the calendar? Your boss is travelling.

It is the season for off-site meetings, be it in another country, state, or province. Ahead of time, find out from your boss about their travelling preferences such as:

- Preferred airline/railway line.

- Preferred traveling time.

- Seat selection (aisle/window).

- Preference for any hotels.

- Do they opt for economy or business class?

- How often does he/she make last minute changes to any existing itinerary?

- If your boss makes last minute changes regularly, I would recommend buying tickets that are one hundred percent refundable or having a minimum service fee for last minutes changes.

- Nowadays most of the senior executive members of any organization always carry a smart phone, an iPad, and a laptop. When your boss is travelling to another country, you will have to arrange for roaming facilities (data and voice). Ask your boss if they prefer to carry either the iPad or the laptop.

Here are some of the most essential details that need to be marked on your boss's calendar about meetings outside the country.

- Ensure the time and duration of the meeting is correct

- Book a cab and arrange for pick up (from office or home). Indicate the cab confirmation number, telephone number, and travel time either from home/office to airport/train station.

- Flight or train booking confirmation details, together with time of departure and time of arrival at destination (round trip).

- Travelling by plane—remember to include the name of the airline, flight number, booking reference, ticket number, and seat number.

- You can print the boarding pass for your boss twenty-four hours prior to the flight and this will avoid them being in the long line at the airport or railway counter.

- Use the airline alert systems to advise either their cell phone or office email address if there are any changes to his/her flight.

- If your boss is renting a car, include the address/telephone number, and contact person of the car rental company.

- Name, address, and telephone number of hotel.

- Hotel booking confirmation number.

- List of some restaurants that are close to the hotel, in case your boss wants to invite some clients for a business lunch or dinner.

- Information on shuttles or taxi services, if they have to travel to their next meeting locations.

- If your boss has rented a car and is driving to the meeting location, print a Google map with the directions for them in case the GPS in their car is not functioning properly.Ensure that all phone numbers and contact names have been updated in his/her contact list.

- Always put the name of the person she is meeting on the subject line. Next to the name add FTF (face to face) or phone meeting if this is a remote meeting. On the location line, add the address and mobile number of the person they are meeting with.

Remember to copy all this information on your calendar as well—(be ready in the eventuality your boss calls and is looking for some details about the hotel's address or the time of the flight).

As you can see from the importance of the calendar, having the correct information in your boss's calendar is essential for their meetings and keeping up with their whereabouts. Detail-oriented Executive Assistants do things better. They generally consider more possibilities, plan better, perform tasks better, and cross more T's and dot more I's. This is where the detail-oriented skill comes in. We all know that most of the time, people like to say—"Think outside the box." However, when it comes to being detail-oriented, Executive Assistants have to "see outside the box." In more specific terms, we find and correct errors, make better reports, and edit documents. Take that extra precaution and the initiative to make sure things become near perfect.

As an Executive Assistant, it is your job to make your boss look good. By simply keeping their calendar up to date, that is one of the easiest ways to maintain a good working relationship. When you do a good job, this reflects on your boss. And when this reflects on your boss, this reflects on you as well, because you are the one who can make your boss proud. You are the one who is going to set things differently, so just be different. Do it well and support your boss in whatever way you can.

Being a detailed-oriented person will make your boss trust you with jobs that need multi-tasking. They will know they can rely on you to make sure and look at every little aspect of any task entrusted to you. Since the trust relationship has already been established between you and your boss, now it's time for you to enhance your detail-oriented skill by paying even more attention to details. See the things that your boss has missed.

Proofread all documents, reports, and emails before they are sent out to other executive members and co-workers within the organization or to external clients. If you are not comfortable reviewing the documents on your computer screen, print a copy. Check the grammar, ensure correct tense of verbs are used, document layout, punctuations, and use the same font and size all throughout the document. Highlight any words that have to be checked against a dictionary to ensure that a good quality work emanates from your boss and from you as well.

Striving to do your best is a sign of hard work and can be a positive trait that leads to excellence. Developing habits and routines really helps you to keep track of the details. Pick out the tiny important details that other people can overlook. Proofread everything before sending out documents to anyone within or outside the organization.

Set up a filing system that can be easily used by your boss, yourself, and for the person who will be your backup whenever you go on vacation for a couple of weeks. Whatever filing system you adopt, it must make sense so that you know exactly where every document is. You have the following options:

Alphabetical – If most of your filings are names of clients, customers, financial institutions, employees, or internal departments.

Subject – If most of your filings are about different types of committees, department meetings, quarterly and annual meetings.

Numerical/Chronological – If most of your filings consist mainly of numbered or dated materials like purchase orders or receipts.

If you have to design your filing system, design it as simply as possible. Show your boss the way the filing system has been set up, because when you go on vacation and there is no one replacing you, it will be easy for your boss to retrieve the files he/she is looking for.

Sweet and simple is the rule of a filing system. Do not exaggerate by trying some kind of fancy filing with doodles on the folders and do not spend too much time figuring out which color of folders you need. The simpler it is, the easier it will be to retrieve any files you or your boss look for.

Also, remember that you can start an electronic filing system. You can make a request with your IT department to create a drive that will be shared by only you and your boss. And that no one else can have access to that drive.

Let me share with you one of the methods I use for electronic filing. I take care of organizing a weekly recurrent meeting, which occurs every Tuesday. Let's call that meeting XYZ Corporate Meeting. Every Monday, I send the following documents to the members: agenda, minutes of the previous meeting, any reading materials pertaining to any items on the agenda. This is how I file my documents for January on the shared-drive. The folder name is January 2014 XYZ Corporate Meeting. Create four sub-folders that I will name differently January 6, January 13, January 20, and January 27. Now in the January 6 sub-folder I will save the following documents: meeting agenda, minutes of previous meeting, reading materials, action notes. If your boss has any hand-written notes for that meeting, scan a copy of the notes and save them in that folder.

You can have hard copy filing and soft copy filing. It is easier to retrieve any documents online. If your boss just wants to have a look at the files online, no need to pull up all the papers and try to retrieve that document. As long as your filing is done in the correct way, it will be easier for your boss to access the shared-drive and browse the documents that he/she is looking for.

Always do follow-ups. This is also a detail-oriented skill. If someone other than your boss gives you highly detailed instructions over the phone about a task that you have to do, I would suggest asking that person to send you an email with the requested instructions. That email with the instructions will give you a solid record to refer to, if some pertinent details escaped your attention while on the phone.

For example, your boss has given you a project to work on and you are very excited to work on it right away. Your first question to them should be, ***"By when do you need this project completed?"*** Do not accept *"in two weeks"* as a reply. Ask your boss for a specific date so that you can plan ahead.

Once you have a guideline on how to tackle different kinds of tasks, such as: proofreading reports, presentations, setting up meetings, or organizing off-site events, it will be much easier for you to find the details that you might have missed.

It is always the little things that set you apart and allow you to display your uniqueness as an exceptional Executive Assistant. Being a detail-oriented person will set you apart; you will see things that others do not see. You will see things that your boss has missed, and this is when you will be portrayed as the exceptional one.

Chapter 4

Efficient

"The combination of hard work and smart work is efficient work."

—Quote from Robert Half.

"I am impressed; you are so efficient, always on top of everything, so organized and resourceful." These are the words of some executives to their Executive Assistants. We all know how important it is to continue striving for success in the workplace. How can we combine both hard work and smart work to become an efficient Executive Assistant? Here you are to the amazing Executive Assistant position and ready to hold down the fort. We all know this wise saying; behind every executive, there is an Executive Assistant who makes business happen. Ask yourself this question: what can I do to help my boss achieve their objectives and what do they expect from me?

How would you know about the objectives of your boss? What does he/she really expect from you? You are not a mind reader. Being an EA, you can have a quick chat with your boss any time you want. Just wait for the appropriate time. By appropriate, I mean a time when they are not too busy, or are just coming back from a meeting with a big smile on their face. If you see your boss with a sunken face, avoid talking to them for about ten minutes, unless there is there is an urgent issue.I think a tip from my previous experience is worth sharing with you. Do you know the first email you receive from your boss in the morning can determine their mood? Yes my friends, this is authentic. Pay attention when you read—if you receive an email without any greetings and a sentence full of question marks, not even a "Thank you"; trust me there is something bothering your boss. Always remember that they have so many things on their plates they are accountable for.Do not start thinking, "Oh maybe I did this wrong or maybe I sent that email to the wrong person . . ." There will be so many "maybes" on your mind and this will just prevent you from thinking clear and you will not be in a position to concentrate on your job.Let us get back to your boss's objectives. You are a newly recruited Executive Assistant; it is your first day at the office. And of course, your boss will be so delighted knowing that they now have someone to support them. If you have not yet done what I am going to tell you, you can do it now because it is never too late. This is how I did it a couple of days after I joined a new organization where I was supporting a Vice President. On a Monday morning as soon as my boss showed up, I gave her couple of minutes to breathe and ordered a coffee, the way she likes it. (The first question I asked her on the day I joined was, "How do you like your coffee?") After that, I went to her office and greeted her with my million-dollar smile, and had a casual chat about the weather. I seized this opportunity and told her that I would like to meet with her that day after the 2:00 p.m. meeting because I am looking forward to knowing how I can help her in achieving her goals. And that if we do not communicate with each other this will not help me to do my job efficiently.

Oh well, this was a productive meeting and after that I set up my one on one meetings with her on a weekly basis. I also asked her to become my mentor as this would encourage better teamwork and she would be in a better position to understand the pressures and challenges that I will be facing in the near future. Being my mentor, she will more likely explain to me more about her decision making on certain subjects and this will give me an insight into her thinking and priorities. This was my first step to success and an example of efficiency.

We have to let our bosses know how efficient and conscientious we are. They can totally rely on us as long as we get their support, and working together in a creative, innovative, and productive manner will bring great results. It is only then you will have the experience and confidence to make decisions and face any challenges cropping up during the day.

Here are some takeaways that you would consider relooking into or adopting.

- Cultivate the habit of always planning for the next day, no matter how tired you feel after an exhausting day. Committing at least fifteen-twenty minutes to establish the next day's plan might seem like a waste of time, but spending the time now, saves time later. Remember to carry over uncompleted tasks to the next day.

- A to-do list is not just a page in your notebook where you scribble your tasks from one to ten or more. Be specific when writing down your to-do list as this will help you to keep track of the things you have to work on. In my chapter on Resources, I am sharing with you a template that I designed and which I am using still today.

- Try to be at the office ten or fifteen minutes early. It gives you ample time to review your to-do list. Sometimes you will have to re-prioritize your TDL (to-do list). For example, last night before leaving the office, your boss left you a message about some urgent presentations that they would like you to work on for their afternoon meeting. In this case, you will not be able to prioritize as per your to-do list and have to change gears.

- Tidy up your desk, it will be easier for you to locate any required document or file. Experience has proven that employees who keep their work areas organized are generally efficient at organizing their priorities. Arrange work documents in a way so they capture your attention, but remember to be very cautious when working with confidential documents. Do not spread out any confidential documents on your desk because you never know who can drop by your place and sneak a quick look.

- Jot down some notes that will jumpstart your thinking and it will help you to start working with minimal delay. When I have to work on an important task, I usually write one or two key words on a sticky note that I stick on my computer screen. Looking at this sticky note when I am at the office in the morning always generates more ideas on what I have to do.

- Be a team player; participate in all activities (if your workload permits). Do your part of the job and do it well. Always keep in mind that your boss depends on you a lot. Do not let them down. Be dependable.

- Be result-oriented. Take ownership if you can and get the task done. Show your boss that you are a "can do" person.

- Always keep your level of energy and enthusiasm high, be fully committed to the organization, its goals, and overall success. Perform effectively with limited supervision and set priorities with minimal guidance.

- Be flexible in accepting new duties, assignments, and responsibilities. Be accountable. Never say, "That's not my job"—always be available to help or offer to help your peers when they are in trouble.

- Take pride in your work. Deliver results because you want to contribute and feel valued and appreciated. Be passionate about your work.

- Learn from your mistakes and by admitting that you were wrong, as this will become a great learning opportunity.

- Share your knowledge, skills, and experience with your peers.

- Develop strong moral ethics. Be honest and respect your boss and peers.

- Be clear, specific, brief, and to the point when communicating to anyone across the organization. Be prepared and avoid rambling conversations and unnecessary information.Check your boss's calendar at least two hours before leaving the office. Do they have any early meetings to attend the next day? If yes, have you already given them the documents they need at the meeting? If there are any lengthy reading materials, I suggest that you give them to your boss at least two days before the meeting, as this will allow them to be prepared and get ready for the meeting.

- If your boss is chairing a meeting, always remember to notify them of any last minute declines by other members.If there is a presentation, ensure the projector and laptop have been set up at least fifteen minutes before the meeting and test to see if everything is working well.

- Are there any other members joining remotely? Make sure that you have provided the correct calling number and participant code. Also, make certain, the correct time zone has been set up.

- If the meeting takes place early in the morning or during lunchtime, remember that you will have to cater for either breakfast or lunch. This is something you must have already taken care of at least two days before the meeting.

- Always have a good sense of humor as this lightens up the day and helps when working through tough situations.

- First thing to do as soon as you reach the office is to check if you have any voicemails. There might be an early message from your boss asking you to cancel the meeting that is starting in fifteen minutes due to an unforeseen priority.

- Check the last email you received after leaving yesterday and the first email of this morning. In my experience, some of the emails that are in your inbox just after you left are somewhat urgent and the first email in the morning is most of the time a follow-up on what was sent late in the afternoon.

- Check your boss's inbox. If there are any emails that you can reply to on their behalf, just do it. But remember to copy them so they know it has been taken care of.

- Before deleting any junk/spam emails, ensure there are no emails related to your boss's work.

- Move any emails with big files to their designated archived folder to free up the size capacity of their inbox. During the day, you might forget about the email that you have moved. In order to keep track of this kind of email, print two copies of the cover email, write a note that you have moved the file to Folder XX, give a copy to your boss, and keep one for your records.

- During the day when your boss is in meetings, make it a habit to check their email every five minutes. You never know when an important/urgent email can land in their inbox and require immediate attention. What would you do if there is an urgent email and it requires your boss's immediate attention? Therefore, this is how I handled this kind of situation once. Print a copy of that email; highlight the important sections. Go to the meeting room, excuse myself to interrupt, and go directly to my boss. Give him the email and leave the meeting room immediately, as I know he will not give me any instructions in front of everyone, considering the confidentiality of that email.

Let me tell you how I start my day each morning. First, I check if there are any urgent voicemails and emails, as these will determine if my to-do list of last night is still good to follow, or if my tasks have to be re-shuffled.

- Do not waste time on irrelevant activities but get right into your job. When you get into the habit of working efficiently, you will be satisfied by how much you have been able to achieve in such a short time-frame. However, you will leave the office feeling productive and successful.

- Put a block to all your personal problems as soon as you step into your work area.

- Before your boss goes away for a long vacation, check if the following has been done:

  - Out of Office (OOO) alert has been activated (emails and phone) and if the OOO has a contact name, phone number and email address.

  - Send an email to the executive members to remind them your boss is going on vacation and will not be available for two weeks. In his absence, Mr. X will hold down the fort, so if there are any urgent issues, Mr. X will be available to help them.

  - Ensure the roaming facilities have been activated if travelling outside the country.

Each day we feel that every single task we have to take care of is a priority. Prioritization is an essential skill that you must acquire. This skill will show you how to make best use of your own efforts. Prioritization is a stepping-stone that will help you to focus your energy and attention to tasks that really matter, to differentiate between urgent, non-urgent, and important. It will help you in assigning your time where it is most required and used efficiently.

Find out which tasks are urgent by establishing goals for each workday. Start with the biggest and most important tasks. Every now and then, we are assigned with tasks that we do not like to embark upon. One of my pet peeves is working on power point presentations, which I have to prepare on a monthly basis for my boss. We all know that we have to start with the biggest and most important task no matter how difficult it is.

Before starting any tedious task, I always work on something that I really like, such as updating the monthly vacations schedule. This self-motivated exercise gives me a boost to start working on the unexciting task. Even if you do not like to perform certain tasks, do not postpone it because you will end up having to rush to get it done, and most likely the end-result will be incorrect.For the sake of example, we will take a routine day's task list. On a routine day, you have eight hours to complete all yours tasks. Here is a list of things to consider:

- Make a list of all major/minor tasks that you have to accomplish.

- Where applicable, break some of the tasks into smaller ones.

- Set target delivery times for each task.

- Make a timetable with a start time and an end time. Include lunch, coffee breaks, reading emails, checking on family and other mundane tasks.

- Assign realistic priorities to each task.

- Identify between urgent and important tasks and label them accordingly.

- Know at what time during the day you are more productive.

- Possess a certain amount of psychic ability. Do not expect specific instructions all of the time.

- Keep abreast of technological changes in the office software environment. An EA is often the first person chosen in an organization to try new technology. It may also be that your boss is not tech-savvy, and you will be the one to whom they will turn to for help.

- Coordinate and maintain your boss' calendar efficiently. Calendars must always be kept updated so that your boss is not overcommitted with too many appointments. Ensure they get to the right place at the right time and have the right documents for the meeting.

- Know how to maintain confidentiality and handle office politics.

Did you know that if you are motivated, your level of efficiency rises?

First, ask yourself about your motivators. What are the things that energize and motivate you when you think about your work?

- To be appreciated—your boss and co-workers congratulating you for doing a good job.

- To have a sense of ownership in your work and the work environment.

- To be recognized and rewarded. To be trusted and respected.

- Flexibility to make decisions.

- Open communication at all levels.

Besides, being motivated will help you to trigger that internal flame within you. This, in the end will take you to your final destination, like accomplishing a very difficult task. There should be a constant awareness of the end-result.

Know the social style of your boss

Every workplace is different. For some it may be an exciting place to go; for others it may be just a subdued place. Often, the difference is in fact a result of the boss. Try to identify early what kind of boss you have and decide how to form the most beneficial relationship with them. By identifying your boss's style, this will help you to become more efficient. Based on some researches, I came to know that there are four different social styles of bosses and each style gives and receives information differently. They are the "analytical," "amiable," "driver," and "expressive." And I will briefly describe each one of them.

1) Analytical-style bosses are those to whom you have to provide lots of information. The more information you provide, the better it is. Analytical bosses are very detail-oriented.Amiable-style bosses are warm, friendly, dependable, and very good listeners.

2) Driver-style bosses want the facts. They want to get straight to the point. They are very decisive and can be very impatient and demanding. Drivers normally want power, control, and authority, and their primary focus is on results.

3) Expressive-style bosses see the big picture. They are not interested in details and are risk takers. They are very loud, personable, and very enthusiastic as well as emotional human beings. They seek recognition.

After reviewing each style of leaders, do your best to figure out which one describes your boss and which one describes you, and then communicate to your boss in his or her style. Identify the other person's style and deliver information to them in their own style to maximize the communication experience for both of you.

Make the difference - Your boss has subscribed to some business magazines, and of course, the magazines are delivered directly to you because you take care of everything for them. Therefore, when you have a chance, this is how you can make the difference. Flip through that magazine; you might see an interesting article that you can share with his/her peers.

No longer than three months ago, my boss has subscribed to a business magazine. Before giving it to him, I just flipped through and came across an article written by one of his peers. To make a difference, I scanned a copy of that article, sent it to his direct reports, and copied him on that email. You know what you can do, but it is more important to let others know what you can do. Organizing effectively is the key to being productive as you can be. Knowing that everything has a place is a sense of relief. When you need something in a rush, you know right away where to find it. You cannot function in a work area that is a mess. Being organized will make your life so much easier, especially when it is very busy. You will know where your things are and they can be easily retrieved.

Be subtle when questioned by fellow colleagues because an Executive Assistant is a resource of confidential information. Pay much attention when talking to anyone across the organization. Always have a poker face when you know some exciting news that will be shared with other employees later. Some studies have found that employees are more productive when their bosses go on vacation. How does your day look when your boss goes on vacation? Actually, this is a great time to catch-up on unattended tasks. Work at your own pace, think of new ideas that will be helpful to you and your boss, re-organize your filing system, and have extended lunch hours or even work from home.

Your first day at the office:

Find out what your boss is expecting from you. Know your boss's favorite type of coffee, any allergies to food, are they on any kind of diet. Try to get pertinent information from your boss, like how they like the filing to be done. Maybe they are comfortable with a certain way of filing, and it is easier for them to retrieve the files when you are not around. If there was not a filing system in place, ask your boss how they prefer the filing to be done. So ask him/her, "How would you like me to take care of the filing?" or "I have my own method of filing, maybe we can give it a try and see if it works for you. And if it does not work, I am very comfortable to adapt to your proposed method of filing."

Your attitude is what distinguishes you and elevates you from being good to exceptional. An attitude to serve and having that burning desire for continual improvement.

Always take pride in doing a job well. When you can do your job with assurance and confidence, your boss will always look good, and you can smile that little smile of satisfaction knowing that you had contributed to making this happen.

Chapter 5

Fearless

"You can conquer almost any fear if you will only make up your mind to do so. Remember, fear does not exist anywhere except in your mind."

—Quote from Dale Carnegie.

Have you ever felt like running away from your desk? Either because you were inundated with work or because you could not wait to go on your first date. This feeling of running away was because of fear. Just by thinking that you might have done something wrong, like misplacing an important file or sending a meeting invite to the wrong person.

We have work-related fears when faced with a challenging task, like working on a presentation that your boss will present at an Annual General Meeting. Fear of being late for work and thinking that this might affect the year-end performance review. Fear that you have been rude to your peer because you were too absorbed in completing a project. Fear to answer the phone on behalf of your boss when you see that the big boss of the company is calling. Fear of having a new boss. Fear of an acquisition. Fear that your vacations are not approved. Fear of rejection when asking for a raise. Fear for being wrong. We all make mistakes, but remember that behind every mistake we make each day, there is a lesson to be learned.

How to be fearless when we have to face certain upsetting situations at the office. For example, your request for a raise has not been approved.

As a result, you will be very disappointed. Accept this refusal as a blessing. Most likely, you would like to talk about this to your boss. So, never put the question like this, "Why was my salary increase refused?" From experience, here is how you should approach your boss. You should say, "I would like to know why I did not meet your expectations. Is there something wrong with my working style? Maybe we can revisit the objectives that were assigned to me and discuss them".

You are finalizing a presentation for your boss when you receive a call from your co-worker asking for help with the printing of some confidential documents. Let your co-worker know that you are busy; offer a brief explanation rather than declining on the spot. Also, let the person know that you will be available after lunchtime and that you will get back to them with a helping hand. You just said "No" in a very polite way and never let the person feel they were let down.

Some executives have very strong personalities. We often tend to be intimidated when they ask us questions. Show confidence and assertiveness in your reply to them. Stop being intimated and be brave. You are wise and you know your job. Make eye contact and watch your body language. Never cross your arms when talking to someone as this sign shows that you are trying to be defensive.

Let me tell you one of my anecdotes. Every time when the CEO calls my boss, the latter is always in his office to pick up that call. It so happened that one day my boss was in a meeting and here rings his phone. As soon as I saw the name of the big boss on the telephone screen, I was already in my panic mode; my heart started thumping, palms sweating. Should I take that call or let it ring—this question was running into my mind. Finally, I answered that call and informed him that my boss was in a meeting. In a very cold tone, he asked me to let him know that he called and to get back to him soon. However, before hanging up he told me not to take a long time when answering the phone on behalf of my boss.

I felt so bad and sounded so incompetent. Feeling bad and sounding incompetent, this was how I chose to feel. Instead, I should have taken that moment as a lesson, so that next time I would be ready for this kind of situation.Everything happens for the best. Make an effort to see the bright side instead of the dark side. Always remember that you are stronger than you can possibly imagine. You can conquer this fear and turn into a fearless person.

Sometimes, we take time to react; we hesitate to take actions, such as replying to an email on behalf of our boss. However, if you feel confident in replying to that email, go for it .We are fearful to take initiatives because we lack confidence; we are uncertain. If you do not want to take the risk to reply to that email, at least prepare a draft, and show it to your boss—this will demonstrate that you are a forward thinker.

Be ready to face and embrace any changes that might happen within your organization. Train your mind to adapt and to acknowledge any changes that you might come across during your career. It will be easier for you to manage any changes, as long as you recognize and accept it. Always be available to take on any new tasks, as this might be an opportunity for you to face new challenges and exceed expectations. You have all the skills to succeed, but you must have the right mentality and the right attitude.

Perhaps you have already lived these experiences about fear or will go through them someday or another. It does not make any sense to be afraid or intimidated. Being fearful will affect your level of productivity and common sense.When you are fearless, you will feel a sense of self-determination, a sense of accomplishment that will make you rise and shine in your job. Remember that fear is a constant de-motivator. You have to be invulnerable to fear and intimidation. You should be bold, ambitious, courageous, and have a strong personal magnetism because Executive Assistants are dauntless.

Chapter 6

Go-Getter

"No person ever achieved success by waiting for someone to hand it to them. Successful people decide they want something and take action to get it. If you seek, you will find. Get going now!"

—Quote from Jeff Bruckner

Do you show up every day at the office? - Everyone is at home and it seems like a great day to skip out of work or you just wake up on a Monday morning and do not feel like going to the office. If you are a go-getter, this idea will never come to your mind. Executive Assistants are go-getters; they are disciplined and determined. They put in time each day to move closer to their long-term goals.

Is this your cup of tea? – If you are passionate about what you do, such as organizing offsite meetings, creating Power Point presentations, scheduling meetings with challenging time constraints, you will look for ways to see that you can deliver a perfectly accomplished task. This is what we call a go-getter attitude.

Are you courageous? – Timidity is not an option and has no place in the mind of a go-getter. Would you be gutsy enough to tell the CEO that they made a typo when sending out a communiqué to all the employees in the organization? Would you dare to do that? However, I did it because I value the image of the company for which I work.

Let me tell you one of my anecdotes—our CEO sent a communiqué to all the employees to let them know that Mr. X, one of our senior executive members, was participating in a major worldwide event. And this event would be telecasted during lunchtime; hence, everyone was invited to get together to watch Mr. X's performance.

The typo made was on the name of Mr. X. Some of you might be thinking that this was not a big deal. But no, I truly thought of this as an important thing and I believe that no one would like to see his or her name incorrectly written. I was debating; should I tell them about the typo or do I forget about it? Finally I made up my mind and walked straight into their office because I figured out how I was going address the typo question. *"Thanks a lot for letting us know about this worldwide event. This is very exciting and we are all looking forward to it. However, I noticed that there is a letter missing in Mr. X's name; just thought that I should let you know".* The moment I was back at my desk, she sent a revised communiqué to inform the employees that the name of Mr. X was not correctly typed. Therefore, if you are going to watch the event, you should be looking for the corrected name. I was so proud after reading this and I gave myself a pat on the back.

Remember that every time we make a mistake, we are learning. Go-getters accept their mistakes and strongly believe that making mistakes will lead them to the route of perfection. Every now and then, we are bound to leave some kind of mistakes in our work. Do not sweat about it too much. Remember that mistakes are inevitable. Always be accountable for your mistakes and learn from your mistakes. I recommend that you jot down all your mistakes in a special notebook that you can call, "My Route to Excellence." Write down in detail about your mistake and how you corrected it. Remember, you are a go-getter, and go-getters are not afraid when they make a mistake. They accept any mistakes they make. Develop your own compass and trust it. Take risks. Dare to fail and remember failures always guide you to the route of success.

Write little notes to ourselves in our calendar. Make your calendar your best friend who will always remind you what you have to do. Never procrastinate. You might be in the middle of doing something, and you just remembered that you have to remind your boss to prepare the speaker notes for his conference in two weeks. There is a big chance that you will forget about it. Stop whatever you are doing. Go to your calendar and write a note to yourself, so that you remember to remind your boss.

Earn respect - You will earn the respect of your co-workers by being a go-getter. They will know you for your dedication, hard work, and consistency in the quality of your work. Be confident in your actions and always try to be a step ahead of others.

Be kind to everyone – Executive Assistants deal with a lot of confidential stuff. For that reason, we avoid mingling with everyone at the office. However, this does not stop you from having small talk with your co-workers and being kind to everyone. Be ready to help, but remember to give credit where it is due. If your co-workers ask you for help, never say that you will not be able to help. Always ask them how urgent it is. Always make yourself available to help anyone in the organization. Above all, give priority to your boss and then take care of the rest. If you feel that you can spare some time to help some co-workers who are stressed out or need assistance, always offer to help. If you know that one of your fellow co-workers has called in sick, offer your help their boss. Your boss will certainly notice your determination to get things done, and this is a go-getter attitude.

If one of your co-workers gave you an idea on how to design a vacation form for your team, thank them for that brilliant idea. Do not take credit for something you did not do, when you implement that new vacation template within your department. Your boss will notice that new vacation template, and they will ask you about that. And this will be the time where you will give credit to your co-worker. Do not take the credit for yourself.

Never give up - No matter how difficult a project is, never give up. Never giving up is the key to achieving success. Fight until the end to get it done. There will always be someone to distract you or even tell you that this project will not be successful. Do not pay attention to their remarks. Focus on what you are doing and see the path of success taking shape.

Take the initiative - Your boss goes on vacation where they will have no access to check emails every now and then. No wonder his/her inbox will be flooded with emails, and there might be a couple of voice messages on their telephone. This is easily taken care of. Listen to the messages and call those persons or send them an email to let them know your boss is on vacation and will be back in two weeks. Ask them if they need any immediate assistance. Someone else will be able to assist them in the absence of your boss. We all have different methods of managing our boss's email. I am sharing with you my method of managing my boss's inbox during their absence. Check email every ten to fifteen minutes to see if there is anything urgent. Any email requiring immediate attention should be forwarded to the person designated as the delegate.

At the end of the day, just go through the inbox once more and see whether required actions have been taken. For those emails that do not require immediate attention, keep them in a folder. Let us say your boss goes on vacation from September 1 to September 15, which is ten working days. How do you manage that inbox which will be inundated with emails? Just pretend they are in the office and do your regular duty. As soon as you are at the office in the morning, check the emails. Knowing that your boss is not here, of course, there will be emails requiring immediate action. What you need to do is send those emails to the person delegated to handle them in their absence. Delete all junk and spam emails. If big files are attached to the emails, save it to the shared folder used by you and your boss. However, remember to flag the email with a note that the file has been saved.

This exercise will be ongoing during those ten days. Everything will be taken care of, and you should bear in mind that nothing should be left unattended in their inbox. Just get going and get everything done. Now that everything is under control, what would you do for them to have an idea what has happened during their vacation? Of course, as the boss, they need to know what has happened and what actions have been taken.

Your boss either works on Outlook or Google mail, so it is easy. I created something very simple to use, and want to share it with you, because it worked very well for both of us. Create ten sub-folders for inbox and sent items. And rename those sub-folders by date so your first folder will be "September 1," "September 2," "September 3," until "September 15." Each mail that you receive at the end of the day, just drag them to their respective folders and flag them. For instance, if you responded to their emails, flag it as, "Replied—see sent items". If there are documents that they have to read, flag it as, "printed/to read." If there are any documents requiring a signature but were not urgent, flag those as, "For your signature."

If you choose to start using the methods above, they will help you to manage your boss's inbox competently. By doing this, you will help them to efficiently use their time once back in the office.

However, most likely your boss will be checking the emails on their mobile device. If this is the case, the flags will not appear on the device; hence, they will not be able to read the notes next to the flags. Prepare a summary in a date format and list all actions taken. Send your summary before leaving the office and call your subject line, "Action taken to emails in your absence."

Actually, using the above method has proven to my boss that I can manage emails in his absence and the sense of trust has been increased.

Do you use the "two-minute rule?" - You can use the two-minute rule when you have replied to very precise emails; such as "Can I have a meeting with your boss on May 12th at 1:00 p.m.?" The sender is very precise in their request. Your reply to that kind of email will be either "yes" or "no." If your response is "no," give the sender a couple of options. Cultivate a mindset that will enable you to be successful in everything you set out to do. Set your mind in a way that there is nothing that can overshadow your drive.

Set targets that you can achieve and ensure that there is some amount of challenge. If you overcome the challenge, you will be inspired to pursue even greater achievements.

Be proactive. Take initiative and be a go-getter.

Chapter 7

Are you wearing your CAP?

"It's not what we do once in a while that shapes our lives. It's what we do consistently."
—*Quote from Tony Robbins*

Do you wear your CAP every morning when you go to work? We all need this CAP, which will help us to fulfill our duty and keep us going throughout the day and all the way through our professional life. I was referring to the three main keys, which I always keep in my pocket. I am giving you these three keys to use, where and when you deem it will help you to unlock the doors of Consistency, Anticipation, and Passion.

Consistency

Having consistency about appropriate attitude, commitment, and performance at work is important in any workplace. Are you consistent? To be consistent you need to stick to your plans and goals. Most likely, you will get off track now and then. When you are lost, get right back on your plan and start moving forward again. All you have to do is to refocus on your goals, revisit them, and see if they are still apt.

Consistency is not only about dealing with your goals; it is also about organizing your working space. At the end of the day, take time to tidy up your desk and make a list of items you must work on the next day. Even if you are working with many files at the same time, do not display them in a messy way. Try your best to organize your desk, because you never know who might drop by, and you would not like the person to see how muddled your work area is.If your work area is in a mess, you will look unorganized. You are creating your own insecurity and you will lose focus. Above all, you will look unprofessional. Try to nurture the sense of consistency to keep your work area as tidy as possible.Being organized helps you to remain calm. You can control confusion. Your productivity will improve, as you will be more resourceful. We all know that having an uncluttered desk creates harmony in the workplace. Always have space on your desk. This will free your mind, and enhance your creativity. If you are well organized and you have everything set up on your desk in a proper way, whenever your boss comes to you and needs a file, it is easy to grab the file, and voila!

Consistency builds trust, because your boss knows that you are dependable. For example, your boss has assigned you to take care of organizing different kinds of meetings for your department.

I will not go into details about organizing meetings. You will schedule the meetings, send out the agenda, prepare the minutes, and mainly follow up on any action notes. You will have to establish a consistent method of following up with the members about topics for discussion at the next meeting and about any action issues they have to look into. By doing this, you have created a reliable work environment; your boss can trust you, knowing that you are capable of working with other members on their team, and that you will not ignore or overlook any task that was assigned to you.

"We are what we repeatedly do. Excellence, therefore, is not an act but a habit."

—Quote from Aristotle.

This is a great quote from Aristotle; reflect on it. Think about the many things that you do at the office. Check emails/phone messages, schedule meetings, organize off-site events, prepare PowerPoint presentations, act as a reminder to your boss (work & personal), travel/hotel bookings, car rental, expense reimbursements—and the list goes on and on. After some time, you start to excel in each of the responsibilities you undertake, because you are repeatedly tackling each one of them and you already have a sense of unique consistency for each single task.

Anticipate

By paying close attention and staying on top of things, you can easily anticipate your boss's needs. If you can keep a step ahead of your boss by anticipating his needs, you will be perceived as the exceptional Executive Assistant. Do not wait for your boss to tell you what to do, take the initiative and do it. Think ahead and be helpful. Never think that a job is too small if it saves your boss's time. When your boss is swamped with work, you can help by taking over routine tasks that they normally handle. Take note of your boss's work habits, try to understand their style and watch how they handle situations and tasks. Keep an eye on your boss's deadlines and if you think that you can help them to beat this deadline, offer your help. If you know how to help your boss, the more valuable you will become. If you know that your boss likes to keep up to date on news related to their respective industry, try to flip through some business magazines and bring any relevant articles to their attention. Try to know what your boss's responsibilities are and if they are currently working on any projects.

Passion

"The only way to do great work is to love what you do"—Quote from Steve Jobs. Show how passionate you are each day when you reach the office and let others feel your passion. Act passionately; beat the deadlines for submitting any projects you are working on.

Passion is one of the key ingredients that will help you to achieve your goals in becoming the exceptional Executive Assistant. Whatever you do, do it with passion. Talk with passion and excitement; let your boss know how passionate you are. And you can do this during your one on one meetings with them.

When you are passionate and committed, you will see how fast the day flies and you will be happy about the contribution you have brought throughout the day.

Chapter 8

Communication Skills

"Communication is a skill that you can learn. It's like riding a bicycle or typing. If you are willing to work at it, you can rapidly improve the quality of every part of your life."

—Quote from Brian Tracy

Communication is just about exchanging messages, be it through a phone conversation, a text message, or writing an email. However, effective communication combines a set of skills that include non-verbal communication and attentive listening.

Listening to your boss & peers - One of the most important aspects of effective communication is listening to others. It is not only about understanding the words or the information being communicated, but also mainly to show respect to the speaker by paying attention to what they say. If the communication breaks down, the sender of the message can easily become frustrated or irritated.

Stop Talking – When your boss is talking, listen to what they are saying. Do not interrupt, talk over them, or finish their sentences for them. When your boss is done speaking, you may need to clarify something to ensure that you have received the message accurately.

Get ready to listen – Since we are easily distracted by other thoughts, we have to put other things out of our mind and concentrate on the message that is being communicated.

Show your boss that you are listening – Nod or use other gestures to show that you are listening and understanding what is being said.

Avoid unnecessary interruptions – Do not shuffle papers or look out the window, as these behaviors disrupt the listening process and send a message to your boss that you are bored or distracted.

Tone of voice - Remember the tone of your voice can be an obstacle or a help to your success. When you talk to your boss, ensure the tone of your voice reflects confidence, assurance, and strength. Never show fear, monotony, or immaturity in the tone of your voice.

Telephone etiquettes are a must when answering the phone

Always identify yourself at the beginning of the call – If you are answering on behalf of your boss, you can say, *"John Smith's office. Good morning, this is Aneeta, how can I help you?"*

Mind the tone of your voice – Do not sound anxious or aggressive. But it is very important that your tone conveys authority and confidence.

Know exactly what you have to say before you place a call – Jot down the items you want to discuss and anticipate that your call might go to a voice mail. Plan your message and be as direct and specific as possible. Remember to state the reason of your call. Always leave your name and contact number for the person to call you back. Also, remember to speak clearly and softly when leaving a message.

Do not get distracted by other activities while speaking on the phone – Rustling papers, chewing and eating, talking to someone else at the same time, or working on the computer can all be distracting. Treat every caller with courtesy and respect.

Email Etiquette

Dealing with emails everyday can take a lot of time. You might find yourself clicking on "reply" and hitting "send" without the attachment you mentioned in your message. Experts agree that our email behavior has the potential to sabotage our reputation both personally and professionally. Here are some tips worth sharing to perfect your email etiquette:

Office matters only/no private stories – We never know how and when a private email lands in someone else's inbox. Sometimes we think we have correctly typed the recipient's name, but this is not always the case because so many people have the same first names within an organization. Therefore, the next time you are tempted to send a personal email, do not use the office email, and instead use your own personal email.

Briefly introduce yourself – Do not take it for granted that the person receiving your email knows who you are or remembers meeting you. If you are replying to your boss's email, remember to include your title at the end of the email or specify that you are the Executive Assistant of Mr. John Smith at the beginning of your email.

Do not send emails when you are angry – Do not express anger in your email. Always remember that email correspondence will last forever.

Use exclamation marks in moderation – One exclamation mark in a business email is sufficient. Too many exclamation marks will make you look childish and unprofessional.

Confidential information – Do not discuss confidential information in emails. If the email goes in the wrong person's hands, you could face serious legal problems.

Respond in a timely fashion – Depending on the nature of the email and the sender, responding within twenty-four to forty-eight hours is acceptable.

Abstain from sending one-liners – "Thanks," or "Okay'" does not advance the conversation. You can put "please do not reply" at the top of your email when you do not expect a reply.

Avoid using shortcuts – When business people use shortcuts to reply to emails, this is not acceptable. For example C U at 3 for the meeting (instead of see you at 3:00 p.m. for the meeting). Do not use smileys, as these look so unprofessional.

Be clear in your subject line – Get to the point in your subject line. Be reasonably simple and descriptive. Avoid typing in all caps or in all lower case because your email will tend to look like a spam email.

Match your message to your subject line – Do not use an old email to send a new message that has nothing to do with the previous email.

Prior to sending large attachments, inform the receiver – Ask the recipient if the inbox capacity will allow them to receive an email with an attachment of over 500KB.

Sending more than one attachment – In your message let the receiver know if you have attached multiple documents.

Send and copy to others – Ask yourself if all the recipients need the information you are sending. Send your messages only to the intended recipients.

Beware of the "reply to all" – Make sure that every member on the email chain needs to know about your message before you hit the "send" key.

Call the recipient instead of explaining, negotiating, or cancelling – When a subject has a lot of factors to be explained, it is better for you to call the recipient. This kind of email will most likely generate many questions and confusion.

Assess the importance of your email – Do not overuse the high priority option. Use the high priority button when a message is really important and urgent.

Maintain privacy – If you are sending a message to a group of people and you need to protect the privacy of your list, you should always use the "Bcc:" field.

Keep your email short and get to the point – Write concisely with a lot of white space to not overwhelm the recipient. Use bullet points to make it easy for the recipient to understand your message. State the purpose of your email within the first two sentences; be clear and be up front.

Always include a signature – If your recipient wants to get in touch with you, always remember to include your signature. When sending an email to co-workers, at the end of your email you can write your name and your office phone extension number.

Remember to activate your out of office message – When you go on vacation, always remember to activate your out of office message. Provide a name and contact number if the sender requires immediate attention to their email.

Your email is a reflection of you – You are what you write; if your email is disorganized and filled with mistakes, the recipient will be inclined to think that you are a disorganized person.

"The way we communicate with others and with ourselves ultimately determines the quality of our lives."
—*Quote from Tony Robbins*

Chapter 9

Resources

"With ignorance comes fear—from fear comes bigotry.
Education is the key to acceptance."

—Quote from Kathleen Patel

I am sure that Chapter 9 will be of great help to you in your daily work. You can print a copy of the resource section and keep it on your desk because you never know when it can be of help to you.

Online Educational Tools	
TED Ideas	www.ted.com
Helpful Video	www.helpfulvideo.com
Videpedia.org	www.vidipedia.org
E-Books and Audio	
Free E-Books	www.free-e-books.net
Audio Books	www.podiobooks.com
Free Audio Books	http://textbookrevolution.com
Writing Tools	
Dictionary	www.onlinedictionary.com
Translation	www.freetranslation.com
Thesaurus	www.thesaurus.com
Encyclopedia	www.reference.com
Guide to Grammar and Style	http://grammar.ccc.commnet.edu/grammar/
Verb Conjugation	http://www.verbix.com/find-verb/
Acronym Finder	http://www.acronymslist.com/

Office Tools	
World Clock	www.timeanddate.com
Calculator	www.online-calculator.com/
Currency Converter	www.xe.com/ucc
Weather	www.weather.com
UPS	www.ups.com
DHL	www.dhl.com
Federal Express	www.fedex.com
Docu-sign	www.docusign.com
Travel	
Airports	www.smilinjack.com/airports.htm
Embassies	www.embassyworld.com
Airline/Hotel/Car Rental	www.travelocity.com www.expedia.com www.kayak.com
Route Maps	www.mapquest.com www.maps.goggle.com
Online Organization/Meetings	
Sandy the Assistant	www.iwantsandy.com
Go to Meeting	www.1.gotomeeting.com
Join Me	www.joinme.com
Professional Clubs	
Microsoft Office	www.office.microsoft.com/en-us/templates
DIY Planner	www.diyplanner.com
Toastmasters International	www.toastmasters.org
International Association of Administrative Professional	www.iaap-hq.org
The Association of Executive and Administrative Professional	www.theaepa.com
Women's Business Mastermind Group	www.womenbusinessmastermind.com

Books to read	
The 7 habits of Highly Effective People	Stephen R. Covey
Who moved my cheese	Spencer Johnson
Eat the frog first	Brian Tracy

TO DO LIST FOR March 23, 2014

Task	For Whom	Priority (H, M, L)	% Complete	Due Date	Delivered on	Copy to	Hard/Soft Filing
Submit February Expense Report	AAAA	H	75%	Mar 31	Mar 28	VVV	Soft

Chapter 10

Believe in Yourself

"Believe in yourself, and the rest will fall into place. Have faith in your own abilities, work hard, and there is nothing you cannot accomplish."

—Quote from Brad Henry

- Imagine it. Plan it. Do it.

- Never lose hope.

- Be confident and happy.

My message to those reading this last chapter is, "Never lose hope and never let a drop of doubt stain your thoughts." If you believe in what you want to achieve, start by imagining your success. Dare to dream your success. Believe in your success. Plan your success. Execute your success and celebrate your successes.

Take at least fifteen minutes of your time on a daily basis to talk to yourself and make peace with yourself. Try to connect to your inside self and let it know about your plans, your dreams, and to guide you to connect with success.

HOPE - This four-letter word is so powerful. If one does not have hope, there is no life. Every day we hope that we will have a fabulous day and everything will be in our favor. Always hope for the best.

Be happy and confidence will follow. As long as you are happy and confident, nothing can prevent you from achieving your set objectives. You have to believe in yourself. I believed in myself and I have written my first book, and this first book is for you. I want to share it with all seasoned and aspiring Executive Assistants.

Believe in yourself. Never lose hope.

- Believe that you are Committed

- Believe that you are Detail-Oriented

- Believe that you are Efficient

- Believe that you are Fearless

- Believe that you are a Go-Getter This gets back to my CDEFGG formula. Take it, work with it, and see how it will help you in your daily life at work.

Believe in yourself because you are the best. Believe in all the chapters that you have read; you will shine and become this extraordinary Executive Assistant.

About the author

Aneeta has worked with Senior Executives at major corporations in North America, knows what it takes to serve as an extraordinary Executive Assistant, and shares the tools, strategies, and principles that make Executive Assistants thrive. Her goal is to give Executive Assistants everything they need to SHINE in the eyes of their employers.

What is the secret to Aneeta's success? Her most important attribute is her "Can-Do" attitude. Aneeta has created the DNA for Commitment, Detail-oriented, Efficient, Fearless, and Go-getter so you too can SHINE in the eyes of your Executive.

Aneeta Pathak lives in Toronto, Canada with two sons, Kayvine and Jay, and her husband Kesh. She immigrated with her family to Canada in 2006 from Mauritius Island where she was born and grew up. She is the eldest daughter of Jay and Maya Oopadhya.

Aneeta started as an Executive Assistant at the age of 19 and has acquired a lot of skills and knowledge since then. Over a span of 3 decades, she has had the opportunity to work in various companies as Executive Assistant. Over those years, she has accumulated wisdom and now wants to help Executive Assistants become outstanding in their careers. Aneeta's byline is "Believe in Yourself" (BIY). There is tremendous power in words that can contribute to one's success.

Trust is a major component of the foundation of successful interpersonal relationships. In the corporate arena, behind every successful Executive, there is an Executive Assistant that makes business happen. Aneeta currently is a Senior Executive Assistant for the Senior Vice President of Insurance at The Empire Life Insurance Company in Canada.

CPSIA information can be obtained
at www.ICGtesting.com
Printed in the USA
BVOW06s0803030217
475040BV00008B/169/P